Subscribe to our pages:
Thegolfdiaries.com &

Be sure to follow us!

Subscribe to:Instagram@thegolfdiaires

FB@thegolfdiaries

Twitter@thegolfdiaries

YouTube@Thegolfdiariesgirl gwen

Contact us at thegolfdiaries.com for information on bulk purchases or speaking engagements. The Golf Diaries can bring the author to your live event.

Smooch
Confused
Not Sure
Worried
Uncertain
Happy
Good
Angry
Dog

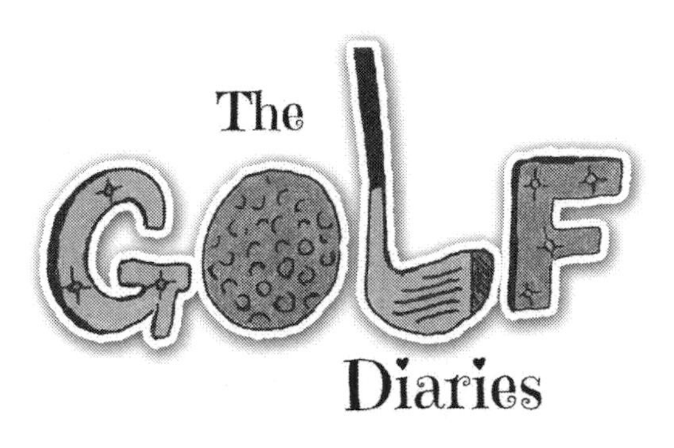

# Castlebetter Academy

Gwen Elizabeth Foddrell

Throughout the book are underlined golf tips and terms.

Publishers Note: This is a work of fiction. Names, characters, places, and incidents are either the product of the author's imagination or are used fictitiously, and any resemblance to actual persons, living or dead, business establishments, events, or locals is entirely coincidental.

Illustrations and Cover design by Gwen Foddrell.



For information on special discounts or bulk pricing contact www.thegolfdiaires.com or email at thegolfdiaries@hotmail.com

**ISBN-13:**
**978-1977715869**

**ISBN-10:**
**1977715869**

This Diary belong to
Chloe Castleberry
a friend of

## Friday

It is July 1, the middle of the golf season is in full swing.

And...my mom has gone off the deep end. Officially!!

She has been reading golf books, watching YouTube videos and looking at training aids.

She says that these efforts will help improve Caleb's golf game and mine.

Seeing her do these things has me scared because my mom can get totally whipped up and it is usually at the expense of Caleb and me.

Caleb came down the stairs for breakfast and we look at each other. I say to him, "I don't know what she is doing but it is probably not going to be good for us!"

I grab a granola bar and start heading to the garage.

As I do I see one of the books she is reading is about a world-renowned golf teacher named David Ledbetter. He started an Academy in Florida and has many top professionals on tour as his students.

I have a feeling the book she is reading has given her one too many crazy ideas!!

I saw Amazon deliver a box to our front porch today that had a big straw type hat in it. Like the one the guy is wearing on the cover of the book she is reading.

My mom then announces she is going to run her own golf academy, right here at our house. She said the name of her Golf Academy is going to be called Castlebetter Academy, as she puts on her straw hat that was just delivered from Amazon!

She says, "Instead of sending us away for a couple of weeks to a camp, she is going to run it right here at our house!"

WHHHHHHATTTTTTT???0!!!

NOOOOOOOOOO!!!!!

This can't be real. I thought this is

what they paid our golf coach for!!!

I ask her to repeat what she said, to make sure I heard her correctly, and YUP, I heard her correctly.

I know she is the QUEEN of DIY but she is taking do-it-yourself to a whole new level.

I come back in from the garage and she is at the computer typing out the schedule for Castlebetter Academy.

Each day she has listed our wake-up time, bedtime, diet, drills, lesson schedule...she even has us doing mental preparations!

She says in her loud, excited, confident voice, "Chloe, you and Caleb are going to LOVE IT and will get better because of it!"

I hope my friends don't find out about this. They will think my mom's the crazy one instead of Mackenzie's mom, Mrs. Maureen!

UGH!

# Saturday

It is a beautiful sunny Saturday. I get up and head to the golf course to get in some early practice.

After hitting balls on the practice range, I walk in the clubhouse because I am thirsty. I see my mom and Mrs. Maureen, Mackenzie's mom, sitting at a table with pen and paper.

WHAT. IS. GOING. ON???!!! Is my first thought.

My mom is taking notes and Mrs. Maureen is laughing and moving papers all around the table.

I have a bad feeling in my stomach!

This can't be a good thing!

Instead of worrying about it I decide to sit down at the table with them and act like I just want to say "Hi". But really...I want to know WHAT is GOING on!

My mom smiles and says, "Oh hey Chloe, you know how I told you I was going to run a Golf Academy at our house for improving your golf skills this summer. Well, Mrs. Maureen is teaming up with me. She is giving me some good ideas on what we can do and is also going to help run some of the course instruction, since she played golf in college. I am so excited about this! It is going to be great!"

I smile, nod, and say, "Ohhh, sounds good, I can't wait."

But in my head I am thinking... *THIS. CAN. NOT. BE. GOOD! I need to warn Caleb ASAP!*

Every time Mrs. Maureen is involved in something it always becomes an intense competition of some sort.

I am finally getting to a good place with Mackenzie after the whole both of us liking Tyler thing.

I don't want golf this Academy thing to ruin the fact that Mackenzie and I are finally real GFF's!

I do not have a good feeling about this whole golf academy at all!

I feel myself getting so mad!!!

I want to scream!!!!

I want to ask my mom WHY!!!

Is she crazy???!!!!

Has she forgotten everything we have

been through with Mrs. Maureen??!! Why would she recruit someone to join her who helps her daughter torture me??!!

I decide to keep my mouth shut, but when I get home, I hope my mom has a good explanation for me as to why she would team up with her.

I look out the window and see Tyler on the putting green, so I smile, excuse myself, and tell them I am heading to the putting green to practice.

The traumatic conversation and thoughts of Mrs. Maureen and Castlebetter Academy make me totally forget that I was thirsty when I went in the clubhouse.

I carry my bag over to the putting green and set it down. I take 2 balls out of my bag to practice putting and drop them on the green.

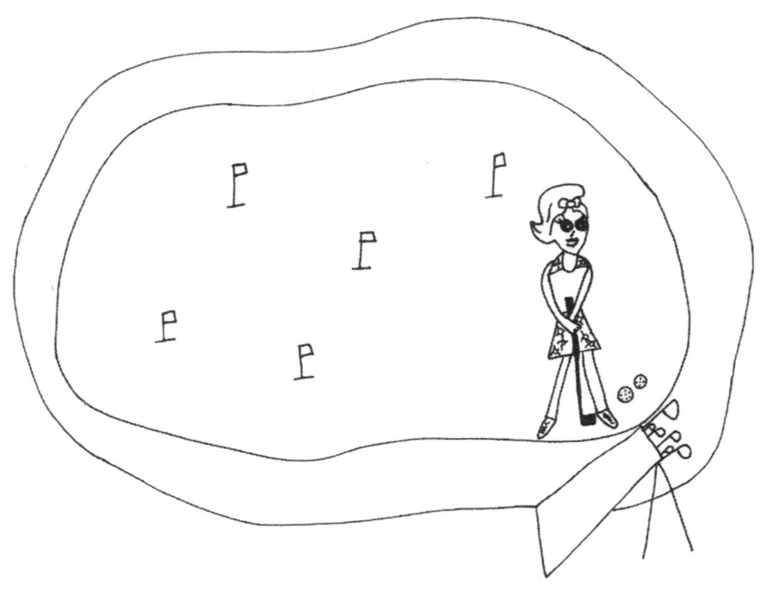

Tyler looks up and says, "Oh, hey Chloe. How long have you been here?" I tell him about an hour. I have been hitting balls on the range and now I am going to putt.

He says, "Cool. I already hit balls, too. Do you want to play nine holes with me?"

I am trying to keep from screaming YESSSSSSSS so in my oh so calm voice I say, "Sure."

We both pick up our bags and head over to the first tee.

It is a gorgeous morning. There is a

slight wind and it is not too hot. But, even if it were 110 degrees outside...I would play and never complain because I am PLAYING WITH TYLER!!!

After we both hit our tee shots down the middle, Tylers' is, of course, a lot further than mine! We start talking as we walk to our balls. He asks me, "How are Putt and Birdie doing?"

I tell him, "Birdie is pure puppy. I can't wait until I can take her to play golf with me but I think I am a long way away from that happening! And Putt is so soft and cuddly! I don't let them play together because Birdie was biting Putt too hard when they were playing the other day. So, now when I get Putt out to play, I have to put Birdie up."

He laughs and says, "Yeah, puppies are not usually calm and behaved. She will grow out of playing rough with Putt, but for now, I think keeping them apart is a good idea."

I then ask him, "When are you playing in your next tournament?" He tells me, "I have one this weekend. I hope I don't get paired with Ray again. Ray is so slow. I have to make sure I take a charger in my bag for my phone when I play with him, because I spend a lot of time on my phone while I am waiting on him to hit his ball."

He pulls his phone out of his bag and says, "Just in case I do have a lot of waiting...stand still." He takes a few pictures of me as we are walking.

Then he flips the camera around and takes a few selfies of us and he says,

"I will look at these pics and remember how much fun I am having with you."

OMG!!!!!!!!!!!!!!!!!!!!!!!!!!!!!
I am soooooo freaking out!!!!!!!!!!

Can this be real???????? I think someone needs to pinch me!!!!

I have a million thoughts running through my head! I didn't want to seem crazy but I want to see the pics he is taking of us to make sure I look good in them.

But I don't want to seem weird by asking for them.

Instead I ask for his phone and take about 40 selfies of me making different faces in each one.

He pops his head in some of them. I am so wrapped up in hanging out with him that I totally forget we are playing golf and about keeping up with the pace of play and it is only the first hole!

The pace of play rule is that it is a group's responsibility to keep up with the group in front. If one loses a clear hole and is delaying the group behind, you should invite the group behind to play through, regardless of the number of players in that group. When a group has NOT lost a clear hole, but it is apparent that the group behind can play faster, you should invite the faster moving group to play through.

We look up and someone is waiting on the tee box for us to hit our fairway shots. There is no one in front of us, but I know with all our selfie taking and talking, we are being slow.

We finish out the first hole and Tyler says, "Lets sit on the bench here and let them play though so we aren't rushed."

I still wonder if I am in a dream. Can he really be this perfect?! I mean he is amazing in every way!!

It makes me feel so good that he wants to take his time while playing golf with me!

And, that he wants pictures of me on his phone so he can look at them later!!!!

I remember when he told Caleb he had a girl friend. IT HAS TO BE ME!!! If another girl saw pictures of me on his phone she would be so mad. I have to be his GGF (Golf Girlfriend)!!!

We sit on a bench, behind the second tee box, with our drivers in our hands while waiting for the two guys behind us to play through.

Tyler asks me, "What are you doing

tomorrow?"

I tell him, " It depends on when my mom starts putting Caleb and I on her ACADEMY SCHEDULE."

I then tell him about my moms "Castlebetter Academy" idea.

He laughs, scratches his head, and says, "I'll tell you what, when I don't have a tournament, I will come, too. And, I will drag Tessa with me. I give him the biggest hug and tell him he is the best!"

In my head I am thinking, ONLY A GOLF BOYFRIEND (GBF) WOULD OFFER TO DO THIS!!!

He IS TOTALLY my GBF!!!

The two guys behind us walk by and say hey to Tyler and thank us for letting them play through.

I could honestly sit on the bench with Tyler all day!!!

I would happily let the next 10 groups play through.

It's Monday! UGH! As I am turning over in bed, just starting to open my eyes, I hear my mom yell from downstairs, "Get up! All the other kids will be here in 15 minutes!"

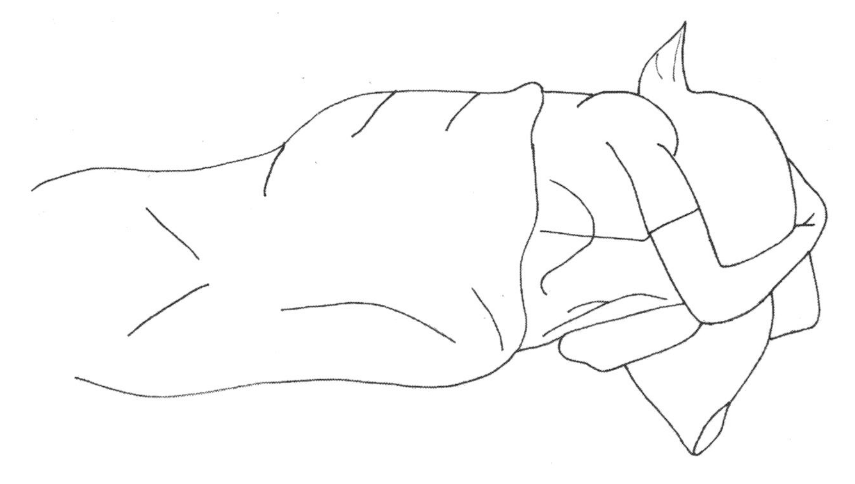

WHATTT!!!!!!

I had no idea it was day 1 of

Castlebetter Academy.

The only thing that keeps me from losing it is knowing I will see my friends. They all somehow got roped in to my mom's Castlebetter Academy.

With Caleb and I included, there are a total of 7 of us at Castlebetter Academy.

I am so happy it is not just me and Caleb!

Mackenzie and her mom are the first ones to show up, and Mrs. Maureen is staying to help today.

When she is not at work, she is going to help run the Academy.

After everyone arrives at our house, we all head to the back porch with our golf bags. We sit on the outdoor furniture talking until the mom's tell us what the agenda is for today.

My mom and Mrs. Maureen are standing in the kitchen talking, drinking coffee, and having a last minute discussion.

They then come outside at 9:15 am and they give us an introduction as to what the next 2 weeks will look like for us.

Mrs. Maureen starts by handing out our academy binders.

Her and my mom put them together.

As they pass them out they also hand

each of us a separate book that is about the mental golf game.

I look up and my mom is putting on a straw hat and is handing one to Mrs. Maureen to put on too.

Honestly, I try not to laugh because I am a little embarrassed about the hats!

I decide to look down at my binder so I

won't laugh and hurt their feelings.

It is so hard to take my mom seriously sometimes.

We all open up our binders and my mom starts explaining how today, and the rest of the Academy, will go.

My mom then explains to us that there are some items that we will be doing on our own every day, like journaling and reading in our mental golf books.

We will have Saturday and Sunday off, but are expected to practice on those days.

The Academy is a total of 10 days, Monday thru Friday for two weeks.

She assures all of us that we WILL be better golfers at the end of the two weeks and we WILL reference back to our Academy notebooks often.

Over the 10 teaching days, we will have a key focus for the day.

Week 1

Day 1 - Grip-Aim-Stance
Day 2  - Putting
Day 3 - Chipping
Day 4 - Nutrition and Hydration
Day 5 – Keeping Stats

Week 2
Day 6 - Driving the Ball
Day 7- Bunker Play
Day 8 – Tournament Rules
Day 9 – Proper Practice Habits
Day 10 - Mental Game

We are also expected to read one chapter each night in our mental golf book and fill out our journal page.

The journal page will cover the topic from the day and have space for us to make some of our own notes.

Mrs. Maureen explained how the journaling will help us to keep focused on our daily goals and chart our progress.

She shows us the journal handout she made:

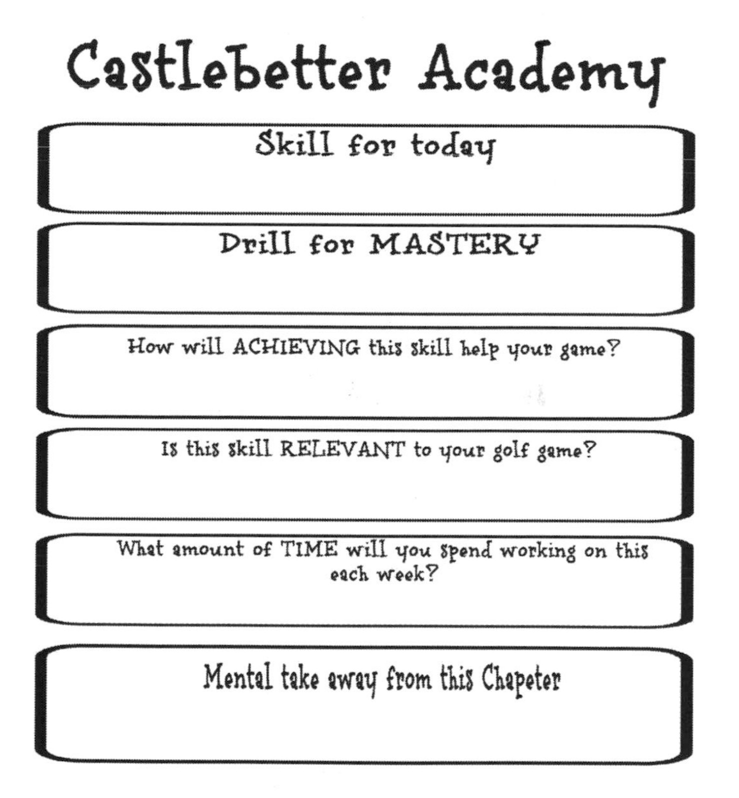
Castlebetter Academy

Skill for today

Drill for MASTERY

How will ACHIEVING this skill help your game?

Is this skill RELEVANT to your golf game?

What amount of TIME will you spend working on this each week?

Mental take away from this Chapeter

I know I will be better at journaling than Caleb. He hates to write down anything. Which, honestly, is probably most boys!

We all close our notebooks and thankfully they are small enough that they fit in the side pocket of our golf bags. We all place them in our bags and head to the course.

When we get there Mrs. Maureen starts by going over GRIP, AIM and STANCE, which is todays topic.

She said it makes the acronym GAS. So you should always check to make sure you have "GAS" before you hit the ball.

# GRIP

She explains to us the things to consider for a good grip. After she goes over them she walks around and looks at each of our grips. She then says the most important take away is to try not to grip the club too much with your palm or you may not be able to hinge your wrists when you swing.

# AIM

She says the most important thing you want is for your body to be aligned parallel with your target line. She walks around and checks our aim.

She then discusses the proper Stance. She says your feet should be shoulder width apart. Your knees should be slightly bent forward and your arms hanging.

Honestly, I had no idea there was so much to think about with your grip, aim, and stance!

It really is a good checklist to run through before you hit he ball.

Mrs. Maureen says going through the GAS checklist will help us develop a more consistent golf game.

Honestly, I quickly realize I am going

to learn so much this week because it is only day one and my head feels pretty full from the grip, aim and stance!

After dinner, I finish up my journaling on grip, aim and stance, and am now lying on my bed reading chapter 1 of my mental golf book before I go to sleep. All of a sudden I hear my phone ding letting me know a text came through.

I look at it and it is a text from Tyler.

SQQQQUUUUUUEEEEEEEE!!!!!!

Instantly, I am not tired anymore!!!
Weird how that works!

I feel jitters in my stomach and I start to smile as I look at the message.
I read it and it says, "What ya doing?"

I wait 2 minutes, so I don't seem to eager, and reply, "Reading my chapter for Academy. How about you?"

He replies, "I tried reading but I couldn't stop looking at the pictures on my phone of us...Saturday was such a fun day!"

I am freaking out! Sometimes I wonder

if he could be any more perfect!

I have the most amazing GBF...I think?!

I honestly don't know if I could have a regular non-golf playing boyfriend.

There is just something about boys that play golf!

Or maybe it is just TYLER. But, whatever it is, I REALLY like him!

I respond to him and say, "You should send me one ;)."

He says, "Alright." And next thing you know, I have a pic of us!!! I LOVE IT!!!!

I am trying to play it cool, but I can't believe he just sent me this and that I am actually having this conversation...with TYLER!!

I then tell him, "I am really exhausted after today. It was so much thinking."

He said, "Things will ease up. The moms are just overexcited right now. We will wear them down and it won't be so intense. lol"

I tell him I hope he is right and then I say something I can't believe I said, I tell him, "I can't wait to see you tomorrow."

He doesn't reply right away. It has probably been 1 minute but it feels like 27!

Then he says, "Me too! Good night, sleep well <3!" And he puts a heart emoji!!!!

SQQUUEEEEEE!!!!!

I wait a minute so I can try to calmly reply and I send back, "Night! <3."

I. AM. TOTALLY. FREAKING. OUT!!!!!

I don't know why but I still am not 1000% sure he is mine. Does he send anyone else a heart? Or just me? UGH!!! I have to figure this out so I don't go crazy!!

OBut, in my heart, I feel like he has to be mine!

I spend the next 10 minutes analyzing

the text message he sent.

I finally decide I am too tired to be logical and turn my phone off and go to sleep.

## Tuesday

It's the 2nd day of Academy and today is putting.

Everyone knows that being a good putter is THE quickest way to shave strokes off your golf score so I am really looking forward to today!

After everyone arrives at our house, we head to the back porch and we see a line of empty water bottles on the table. On each bottle is each persons' name written in black sharpie marker.

I have no idea what these are for!

My mom instructs us to each take the empty water bottle with our name on it and start walking toward the golf course to the practice putting area.

When we arrive at the practice green,

my mom explains to us that we are going to play a putting game. She said, "Everyone is going to play the putting game with the water bottle under their right arm, since you all putt right handed."

She calls us over and has us watch a short Ledbetter video from YouTube on her phone. In the video, Mr. Ledbetter explains how this drill helps your arms and shoulders move together as a unit.

We each place our empty water bottle under our right arm.

We then apply slight pressure to the water bottle and practice our putting stroke.

My mom reiterates that this will help us make a stronger, smoother putting stroke.

It will cause us to use our arms and chest as a unit when putting, which makes for a better rolling ball and a more predictable putting stroke.

In golf, predictability is EVERYTHING!!

We are all hanging out on the green practicing with the water bottle before we start the actual putting game.

I must admit it feels weird, but it does make it easier to keep the putter path straight, and the ball makes a nice clicking sound when you hit it.

My mom then called us over to the side of the green and explained the rules for the worst ball putting game.

She explains, "You take two balls. You putt both toward the hole. The ball that is furthest away, your worst ball, is the one you must play. But, you must hit both of your balls from the worst ball spot and make them both to not get a point added to your score. And the lowest score wins."

It sounded easy enough. As we started to break into groups, it seems Julie is always standing right by Tyler. And today was no different.

Julie quickly asks Tyler to be her partner.

Honestly, HE IS THE BEST PUTTER! She knows she has no chance against him. She knows she will lose! I don't know what she is thinking!!

He is always so polite and nice so he tells her, "Of course."

I know he would rather be playing with one of the boys.

I asked Mackenzie to play with me. I have fun hanging out with her. She is so funny because she says the things that everyone else is usually thinking, but too afraid to say.

She then looks over at Julie and I hear her say, "Julie, you have no chance against Tyler!"

At that moment, I LOVE MACKENZIE! I feel like she is standing up for me.

I learned that being allies with Mackenzie is where you want to be.

Mackenzie then says, "Julie, there is an odd number since there are 7 of us. You play with Tessa and let the three boys play with each other."

Mackenzie is such a take-charge person and I love her. And at this moment, I know Tyler loves her too.

Tyler hears her and quickly says, "Good idea Mackenzie!" And he walks over to join Caleb and Scott.

## Wednesday

This morning, while I am waiting for everyone to arrive, I get my binder and look ahead at todays' agenda. It says we are chipping.

Castlebetter Academy- Wristless Chipping

*Ball in the back of your stance with a narrow stance.
*Weight on front foot and leaning slightly forward.
*Rotate chest back and come through the ball much like a putting stroke.

Once everyone has been dropped off at our house, we start to walk over to the practice area together.

As we are walking I quietly say to Caleb, "Today is mom's $5000 shot!"

Caleb replies with, "Oh great! Nothing wrong with the technique but mom's "in your face" comments and puffed-up chest about her results are annoying!"

I agree with him and say, "I just hope she doesn't embarrass us today!"

I think to myself, *everyone else has no idea what a treat they are in for today!*

I am hoping when we arrive at the

course that Mrs. Maureen will be there and will tell us she is running the drills today.

NO. SUCH. LUCK!

We arrive at the practice green and first thing I see and then hear is my mom. She is wearing her big hat, standing tall with a smile on her face, and talking about her $5000 shot.

She calls us all over and then explains, "Everyone, I am here to let you know that today I am sharing a $5000 GOLF TIP WITH YOU!!"

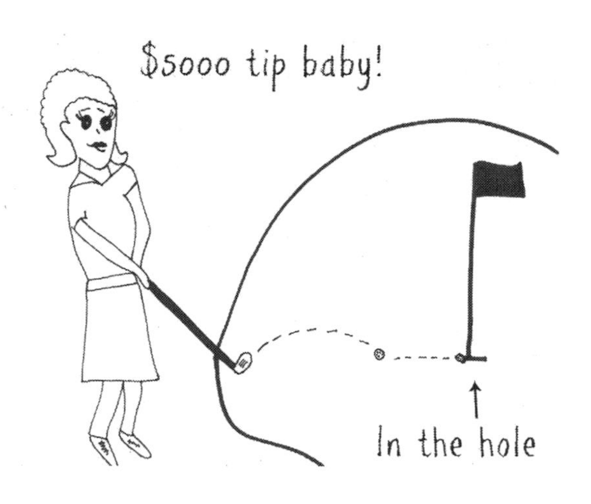


I try to stand behind Julie so I can hide. I don't want to be a part of this!

I mean, I will admit it has helped her. She shot her best round of golf on 9 holes the other day and it was because of this shot.

But, I am dreading all her theatrics that go with her love for this shot.

Okay. So, as it turns out, today wasn't as bad as I thought it would be.

And everyone really seemed to like the technique and felt it helped them chip their ball much closer to the hole.

Even Tyler admitted he uses this shot for his short game and he can consistently get the ball within 5 feet using the technique.

After hearing Tyler say he is using it, I decide that maybe I need to not be so afraid of what my mom might say or do. I really need to focus on trying to listen and apply some of the things she has studied and put together for the Academy.

I know my mom does a lot of research and has put in lots of time preparing for our summer Academy. I think I am going to try to have a better attitude about everything.

I mean if Tyler is using it, it has to be good because he is such a good golfer!

## Thursday

Today is a lighter day. We are reviewing everything we have done but also discussing nutrition and hydration.

Food and drink seems like such a simple thing, but it honestly takes quite a bit of planning for me when I am playing golf.

I forget to eat and drink until I get a headache. When my head hurts, I tend to play a little careless.

We got a handout that went over hydration during golf, eating before the round, eating during the round, and recovery from the round.

My mom went over what different LPGA and PGA players eat before, during, and after a round.

To be honest, I really only remember the info on MY RICKIE!!!!

Rickie Fowler said in the morning he eats some sort of eggs. After a round, if he had the choice, he would eat chicken, rice, and broccoli.

OMG!!!! My favorite meal is chicken,

rice, and broccoli!!!!!!

We are meant to be together! I really like Tyler BUT "MY RICKIE" is #1 in my heart!

I mean how can he not be. He is such an amazing golfer and person!

And...amazing to look at too!!!

I just know that one day we will eat chicken, rice, and broccoli together!

I just know it!

## Friday

It is the last day, of the first week of Academy, and the topic for today is course management.

As everyone arrives at our house, I am thankful to see Mrs. Maureen is here today!

I love my mom and all, but Mrs. Maureen knows more about course management than my mom and it helps to have someone with competitive tournament experience and not just

YouTube videos.

It is the last day of the first week of the Academy, and the topic for today is course management.

As everyone arrives at our house, I am thankful to see Mrs. Maureen is here today!

I love my mom and all, but Mrs. Maureen knows more about course management than my mom, and it helps to have someone with competitive tournament experience and not just YouTube videos.
Mrs. Maureen starts out the day by

going over the importance of us keeping our own stats.

She explained to us how keeping stats will help us with damage control on the course. She says, "It helps you make different decisions when you have difficult lies or shots you are facing."

She then told us how her college golf coach, during her college golf matches, made all the girls on the team keep their own stats for each round they played.

Mrs. Maureen told us, "At first it will feel a little overwhelming, but you will get used to it, and then it is no big deal. The information you gather is so helpful that it will make it hard NOT to keep your stats once you start doing it."

She then showed us how to take a regular scorecard and label it for the stats you are keeping for the round.

| HOLE | 1 | 2 | 3 | 4 | 5 | 6 | 7 | 8 | 9 | OUT |
|---|---|---|---|---|---|---|---|---|---|---|
| PAR | 4 | 4 | 4 | 5 | 4 | 5 | 3 | 4 | 3 | 36 |
| | | | | | | | | | | |
| | | | | | | | | | | |
| | | | | | | | | | | |
| | | | | | | | | | | |
| | | | | | | | | | | |
| | | | | | | | | | | |

Regular Scorecard

She explains, "You need to write your name on the scorecard and then in the slots below, where other names would go, you write the abbreviations DIF (drives in fairways), GIR (greens in regulation), SS (sand saves)/Up & Down, and Putts."

| HOLE | 1 | 2 | 3 | 4 | 5 | 6 | 7 | 8 | 9 | OUT |
|---|---|---|---|---|---|---|---|---|---|---|
| PAR | 4 | 4 | 4 | 5 | 4 | 5 | 3 | 4 | 3 | 36 |
| | | | | | | | | | | |
| Chloe | | | | | | | X | | X | /7 |
| DIF | | | | | | | | | | /9 |
| GIR | | | | | | | | | | / |
| ss/↑↓ | | | | | | | | | | |
| Putts | | | | | | | | | | |

She continues to explain, "You will put the correct marking in the column that coordinates with the hole you are on. These are good basic stats to start with. After you finish each hole you will put either a check mark, X or a number. The check mark means YES you did hit the fairway off the tee, or you did hit the green in regulation, or you did make your up and down or a sand save. The X means NO you didn't make the goal. For the sand saves and up and downs you only put a mark if you have a sand shot or an up and down."

| HOLE | 1 | 2 | 3 | 4 | 5 | 6 | 7 | 8 | 9 | OUT |
|---|---|---|---|---|---|---|---|---|---|---|
| PAR | 4 | 4 | 4 | 5 | 4 | 5 | 3 | 4 | 3 | 36 |
| Chloe | 5 | 4 | 4 | (4) | 5 | 6 | 3 | 5 | 3 | 39 |
| DIF | X | ✓ | ✓ | ✓ | ✓ | X | X | X | X | 4/7 |
| GIR | X | ✓ | X | ✓ | X | X | ✓ | ✓ | ✓ | 5/9 |
| S/S | | / | / | / | / | / | / | / | / | 1/2 |
| Putts | 2 | 2 | 1 | 1 | 2 | 2 | 2 | 3 | 2 | 17 |

The golf term "up and down" refers to the act of taking just two strokes to get your golf ball into the hole when your ball is resting around the green or in a greenside bunker within a 50 yard range. If you accomplish this, then you've achieved an "up and down".

Mrs. Maureen told us after her college team kept their stats for a few weeks, they quickly realized that the whole team was weak in hitting the greens in regulation.

Upon taking more detailed stats, they determined that they were consistently falling SHORT of the greens.

Her coach took this information and made the entire team club up. They were not allowed to club back down until they hit the ball off the back of the green at least 3 times.

She said that once the girls clubbed up

they were all scoring better.

Clubbing up means you take more club (meaning longer distance) and clubbing down means you take less club (shorter distance).

Mrs. Maureen then passed out a PWCC scorecard to everyone. She had us each write down the stats we were keeping for today.
She said, "You are going to pair up and play 9 holes. Boys in one group and girls in the other. And, club up going into the greens. The only way you can club back down, to what you think is

your normal shot into the greens, is if you hit 3 shots off the back. Then you can club back down."

We are going to have so much fun playing today! I can't wait.

My mom then tells us, "Get your bags and head over to the first tee."

As we are heading over to the golf course the sun is shining right in our eyes. I hear Julie say, "I forgot my sunglasses!"

I usually carry an extra pair in the zip pocket of my bag. I paused first to see if anyone else had any to loan her and they didn't.

Since she is my GFF...I told her the ones I have on are my absolute favorite but she could borrow them and give them back to me when we are finished...since we are GFF's.

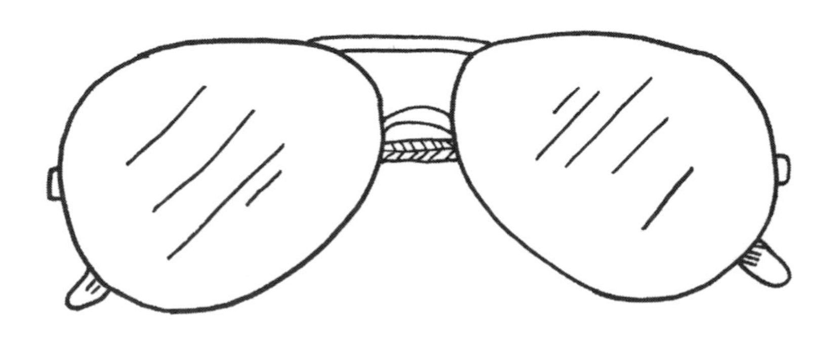

Julie replied, "OH, THANKS!"

She snatched them right off my face and bounced off like she was the Queen of the world!

She then took her phone out and looked at herself with the selfie screen and said, "I love them!"

I smiled at her, then reached in my golf bag and got my other pair out of the zipper pocket of my bag.

I love Saturday because I get to sleep in!!

Once I wake up, I like to lay in bed, turn on my phone, and start scrolling through my Instagram.

First thing I see on Instagram is a picture of Julie wearing MY SUNGLASSES in her car and she captions the pic, "HEADING TO THE BEACH!"

To be honest, I totally forgot to get them back from her, but that is beside the point.

Why didn't she give them back to me!!!

I can't believe:
1. She still has them and
2. She is wearing them AND taking pictures with them BUT
3. SHE IS POSTING PICTURES OF HERSELF WEARING THEM ON INSTAGRAM!

They weren't expensive sunglasses but she doesn't know that!

Honestly...it is just rude!!!

I wanted to remain somewhat calm and not comment right away about giving them back. But, I do want them back...terribly, since I love them so much.

I guess with the craziness yesterday at Castlebetter Academy I was so overwhelmed with our stat taking that I totally forgot about asking for them back.

So I commented on her photo and said, "Haha love the sunglasses!" I was hoping that she would say OH YEAH, I will give them back to you when I see you!

But nope, she says, "Thanks! I love them too and I have gotten so many complements on them already!"

Which was not the answer I was looking for!!

I asked my mom what to do and she said, "First of all, don't lose a friend over a $6 pair of sunglasses. Second, ask for them back and give her a chance to return them before you get upset."

She did also suggest I wait until Monday morning to ask for them back.

She said, "When it is about time for her to leave to come to our house, text her and ask for them back."

I thought this suggestion was brilliant! That way she can't say she FORGOT!!

I know my mom is right but I am still so MAD AT JULIE!!

And I know it has only been 1 day that she has had my sunglasses, but it feels like it has been a whole week!

Probably because I have already seen a weeks worth of pictures with her wearing them!

## Monday

So yesterday, Sunday, I saw 3 more posts Julie made of HERSELF in MY sunglasses!

So, since it is Monday morning, I am getting ready to text her to ask her to bring my sunglasses back. I check Instagram real quick and I see she posted on her Instagram story, "Broke my phone!" ☹

That's not what I wanted to see!

But, I am glad it is not MY SUNGLASSES that are broke!

I am wondering if she is only saying this so I can't message her to get my sunglasses back!!!

My first thought when I saw her story on Insta was, *well isn't this convenient!*

So, I thought about it and decided to text Julie's sister, Josey, since I REALLY wanted my sunglasses back.

I texted Josey at 8am since Academy was at 9am.

My text simply read, "Hey Josey, I saw Julie broke her phone. Could you ask her to bring my sunglasses back when she comes to the Academy this morning?"

Josey replied, "Okay let me ask her." Which I was thinking...*Okay. Fine. Whatever!*

I don't know why she has to ask her whether or not she can give MY sunglasses back.

Especially since I know she has them and she wore them everywhere she went over the weekend. Knowing they are MINE!

But, I just said, "Okay" and I waited for her to respond.

She responds and texted, "Julie said you gave them to her and they are now hers." My stomach dropped when I read this and I wanted to scream and go crazy because not ONCE did I say to her, you can have them.

I remember I specifically said to her, "You can BORROW them for today and you can give them back when you leave."

So, I am trying to calm myself before I reply, "No, I told her she could borrow them for the day, not keep them."

She responds and says, "Okay" with a mad face emoji.

I can't believe she would be mad at me because I want her to give MY sunglasses back when they are MINE, not hers!

And, I think the only reason she likes them is because THEY ARE MINE!

And yes, they aren't expensive or name brand, but I got them on vacation.

They were the last pair, and I haven't seen any more like them and I just really want them back!!!!

So, I don't respond and decide to just leave the situation alone.

When Julie arrives to Academy, she walks in and hands me my glasses and seems totally fine but then walks over to talk with the boys, which is not a normal behavior for her.

I thank her for bringing them and she just nods.

Mrs. Maureen starts talking and announces that today at the Academy we are going over the driver.

To be honest it is a good day for the driver because all I want to do is pound balls as hard as I can because I am still a little upset.

Fortunately, as the day went on, Julie seemed to normalize some.

I am glad everything got resolved and I

know we are still GFF's, but I still think the whole "keeping the glasses" situation was weird!

## Tuesday

This morning I woke up a few minutes early, so I picked up my phone off my nightstand, and I scrolled through my Instagram feed while in bed.

I see Julie's phone is working now and she made a post on Instagram ranting about fake friends and how people really betray you.

I know she is directing this whole post at me!!!

Which I think is ridiculous because she is fighting with me over MY $6 pair of sunglasses.

Which, by the way, I thought was over since she gave them back!

After seeing her fake friends post, I am honestly a little nervous about the Academy today.

I wonder if: 1.She is coming 2.She is all mad and 3.She is mad it is going to make for a long day!

I head downstairs to eat breakfast. When I finish eating I go to my back porch and wait for everyone to arrive. We usually start at 9:00am. I look at my phone and the time reads 9:25am and we haven't started yet. I realize everyone has arrived at my house for the Academy, EXCEPT JULIE.

So we are all hanging out, waiting until she arrives.

I keep glancing down my driveway for her and I finally see their car pulling up. My heart starts to pound because I don't know if she is going to be nice, act like nothing happened, or be mean and confrontational.

Then I think to myself, *I don't know why I am even worrying. Everyone here witnessed me LOANING her MY sunglasses!*

When she gets out of her car and walks around to the back porch, I try to not have eye contact with her.

Mackenzie waves to her and says, "Hey Julie!" Then we all, as a group, picked up our golf bags and start walking to the golf course. As we are walking Julie seemed angry just by her walk.

I decide to keep to myself and think about today's Academy topic. Today, Mrs. Maureen is going over bunker play.

When we get to the course, she first went over how to stand for bunker shots.

I was listening, but out of the corner of my eye I was trying to watch Julie to see how she was acting.

When Mrs. Maureen told us to head over to the bunker practice area, Julie came over and walked with me, Mackenzie, and Tessa. She actually was very nice and normal...thankfully.

We ended up all talking and laughing and slinging sand everywhere today. It was a lot of fun!

I guess things ARE back to normal, at least it feels that way...but honestly, who knows.

I do know, however, that GFF's can be dramatic!!!

My personal lesson for today is to always stay calm in what feels like upsetting moments. And to not say anything I will regret because you never regret the things you didn't say and in the end, everybody should remain friends.

After all...WE ARE ALL GFF'S!!!

# Wednesday

Today, "The Moms" worked together and took turns going over some of the most common rules faced in a golf tournament.

Rules are not very exciting but I understand they are something we all need to know.

The basic tournament rules they covered today were:

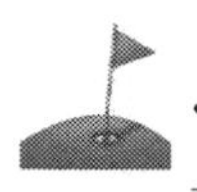

# Teeing Ground

Rule 11-3 Ball falls off the tee or knocked off by something other than the golf club. - NO PEALTY

Rule 11-4 Ball is played outside of tee markers. 2 STROKE PENALTY (You can play the ball a maximum of 2 club lengths behind the markers.

## Ball Placement on Tee box

Or Behind
By up to
←
2 club
lengths

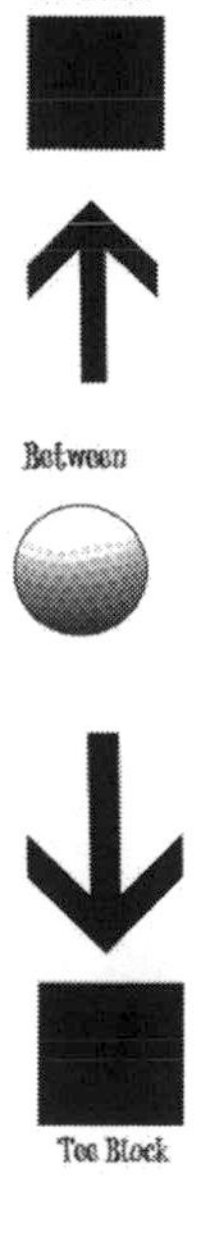

# Out of Bounds

# (White stakes or line)

**Rule 27-1** If you hit the ball out of bounds, play the ball again from the same spot the original ball was last played. 1 STROKE PENALTY

**Rule 27-2** If you are not sure your ball is out of bounds or will be able to locate it, play a provisional ball. Make sure to declare to your group that you are playing a provisional ball(VERY IMPORTANT). NO PENALTY

If you forget to declare it as a provisional ball, the provisional ball is now in play regardless of whether or not you locate your first ball. 1 STROKE PENALTY

# Lost Ball

Rule 27-1 You have a maximum of 5 minutes to look for your ball. If you can't find it, it is lost. You must play the ball again from the same spot the original ball was last played. 1 STROKE PENALTY

# Ground Under Repair

Marked with stakes, ropes, or typically white paint. You

get a free drop out of the area. NO PENALTY

## Ball Unplayable

Rule 28 - You can decide that a ball is unplayable at any place on the course except when the ball is in the water hazard. 1 STROKE PENALTY

Options:

A.) can replay it from the original spot.

B.) You can play a shot as far back as you want as long as the dropped ball is in line with the hole and the point where the ball last laid.

C.) drop a ball within 2 club-lengths, no closer to the hole

## Water Hazards

1. Find out if you are in a lateral water hazard (Red stakes or line) or a water hazard (Yellow stakes or line).

2. Look to see if there is a drop zone. (Usually circled)

Rule 26-1

Water hazard options (Lateral Water Hazard 3 options / Water Hazard 2 Options)

A. You can replay it from the original spot

B. You can play a shot as far back as you want as long

as the dropped ball is in line of the hole and the point where the ball went into the water.

C. Drop a ball within 2 club-lengths, no closer to the hole.

Option 'C' is only available for lateral water hazards.

## Additional Rules

Play 2 balls through the hole if you are not sure of a ruling. You can get clarity on the ruling from the Marshal before you sign your scorecard.

If you hit and hit the ball more than once? Just add a penalty stroke for a total of 2 strokes on that swing.

A penalty relief is 2 club-lengths, a free relief is 1 club length.

When you make a drop, you can NEVER be closer to the hole.

**I know rules are not exciting, but so important to know!**

After "The Moms" went over these rules we all walked to the first tee box. "The Moms" had us draw straws and told us that we were going to play a 9-hole match against each other.

The short straws are one team and the long straws are the other team.

The groupings after drawing straws were:

Tyler, Mackenzie and I are in the first group. We drew the long straws.

Caleb, Scott, Tessa, and Julie in the second group. They all drew the short straws.

Honestly, I am so glad I get to play with Tyler and Mackenzie today, but only because I really do think Mackenzie is over him. So, this will be so much fun...I am hoping!

In today's match "The Moms" explained that we score points by calling rules infractions. The individual with the fewest broken rules wins.

To make sure that we will all call each other out, the moms announce that they have a prize for the winner. It is a $50 gift certificate to the PWCC golf shop.

The minute the prize is revealed the boys all start talking about what each of them will buy with it when they win.

The conversation between the boys quickly shifts to a discussion of golf balls, putters, and golf clubs. I have a feeling the girls are in trouble.

On the first tee we all started out

very relaxed and things seemed fun. Then I realize...I am playing with the best youth female and male golfer at PWCC. This might not stay fun and has the potential to get very heated!

Boy was I right! By the second hole Mackenzie and Tyler were raising their voices at each other and calling all kinds of rules infractions on each other.

To be honest there were some things I had never even heard of! They both have a lot of tournament experience so I know they both know what they are talking about but the things they were arguing about seemed ridiculous. For

example, Mackenzie was getting on to Tyler about how he marked his ball on the green, and Tyler was getting on to Mackenzie about how she placed her ball back after she marked it.
I didn't see any of what they were talking about.

All I know is, what I thought was going to be a fun round of golf turned out to be a round of "I can't wait until this is OVER!"

After both groups finished the 9 holes we sat in the clubhouse waiting to see who won.

It was a little tense between Mackenzie and Tyler. I was hoping I wasn't going to have to speak up for either one of them about the rules they called on each other. But fortunately neither Tyler or Mackenzie won.

Caleb won!

He was playing with Julie, who didn't know the rules very well, and he won by a landslide!

I am honestly glad neither Tyler nor Mackenzie won because it keeps me from having to pick sides with them.

All I can say is PHEW! Glad today is over!

## Thursday

Today, "The Moms" have a meeting they are going to attend that is about our up and coming overnight girls golf camp. Tessa, Mackenzie and I are attending it in 2 ½ weeks and I can't wait!

Since both "The Moms" are going to be gone from the Academy today my mom asked my dad to fill in.

My dad said he would fill in for today but was NOT going to wear the straw hat.

Today's Academy topic is proper

practice habits.

My dad told us to start with hitting some balls on the range and he was going to observe us.

He paced back and forth along the range and watched us practice.

After 2o minutes, my dad stopped us, called us all over and told us Tyler was practicing correctly and he wanted to help everyone else have a more effective practice session.

He said, "Practice and warming up before a round should not look the same. The majority of what I am watching looks like someone who is warming up to tee off."

He said, "You all are rifling through the clubs in your bag like you are getting ready to play a round of golf. Professionals never practice that way. They will take one or two clubs and work on mastering a shot."

He then gave us an example of how a professional might take an 8 iron and work on hitting it straight, high, low, draw or fade. They will work on really getting down certain shots with a certain club.

Well this is the first time I have EVER heard this!

I mean, I can see how this would be beneficial, but I didn't know this was how to practice before today.

I always go over and start with my wedges and make my way to my driver.

He said he wants us to each pick one club and for the next 20 minutes work on a specific shot with it.

And for the next week we are to work on one iron or wood, one chip shot, and one putting drill in each practice session.

He then took us over to the putting green.

He watched us practice our putting for about 5 minutes. He called us back in and told us all to only take one ball on the putting green to putt with.

He said that way we are simulating real play.

It will also help us to put more thought into each practice putt.

He said a good exercise is to play 18 holes on the practice-putting surface with one ball and try to shoot for a total of 30 putts or less. He said we should do one long putt, then one short putt. Long is 20-30 feet and short is 5-10 feet.

I am glad my dad was here today and told us all this! He has a lot of knowledge. But honestly he should because he has read every golf magazine for the past 25 years, cover to cover!

But, his knowledge was helpful today because today is the first time I had ever heard of how to practice!

After working on putting we took a water break. After the water break we all went back over to the range to hit balls for the last hour.

All of us were practicing very different than how we were before.

I really felt like I was working on something other than just hitting balls!

It felt good!

It felt like I was more intentional which made me feel like a better golfer.

Thanks Dad!

## Friday

Last day of Castlebetter Academy is today!

Once everyone arrives at our house, we go over to the driving range. Once we are at the range my mom tells us today's topic is the mental golf game.

She announces to everyone, "We will start the day with a nerve calming drill, and then in the afternoon we will be meeting with Chloe and Caleb's Papa, for some mental golf coaching."

I am really looking forward to today because sometimes, no matter how hard

I try to think positive, I can't get myself feeling good before hitting the ball.

We started out with a drill that is for "feeling" better about your ball striking.

You take your favorite wedge and make a waist high backswing and a waist high follow through. This drill is commonly used for high handicappers but it can really help you get a good crisp feel for good ball striking.

My mom explained to us how getting that "good feeling" can help you calm your nerves when you feel you are not hitting the ball your best.

After our morning practice we took a longer lunch break because it is the last day of the Academy. When we finished our lunch we went over near the clubhouse to meet with my Papa.

He had us all sit under a tree in the shade as he began talking to us.

He told us, "The world today is so fast-paced and results-oriented that it's hard to stay 'in the moment' and focused on what you're doing while playing golf. In a round, the tendency is to look ahead or dwell on holes you've played. Both of those situations clog your brain with distracting thoughts."

He then continued and told us, "If you have trouble putting mistakes behind you, it's time for a reality check. Many golfers are shocked by the errors they make; for instance, you might top a drive and focus on it for three holes. If this sounds like you, look at your track record. If you occasionally top the ball, don't be blown away when it happens in a round. Stick it in the back of your memory as something to work on and play your next shot."

I so needed to hear this! I loved today!

I love the thought of not expecting perfection in golf.

When I was figure skating it was all about perfection.

And it was soooo stressful!!! I love that he is telling us to NOT expect perfection and TO expect to mess up and be okay with it!

As much as I love that messing up is okay and that I don't have to be perfect, my favorite take away I had from Papa's talk was when he was talking to us about staying present in our golf round.

I really need to work on this. I always have one or 2 holes on each 9 where I stop focusing and seem to be anywhere but on the current hole I am playing. I am going to really work on trying to stay present for my whole round.

Thank you Papa!!!!

.

# Saturday

So, I am starting to question my GFF relationship with Julie.

First she took my sunglasses at the Academy.

Today she is texting me and telling me that she has been texting Tyler. She said she is totally crushing on him and she thinks he feels the same about her.

She said that they are going to wear matching socks at the golf course.

She said they have gotten so close through texting and by being paired up at the Academy, and then she put a bunch of heart eye emoji's and laughing faces.

I just sent back laughing faces to her and tried to act normal. But in my head I am thinking, *is she competing with me? Trying to upset me? I know she knows Tyler and I like each other! Why*

*would she do this?*

I can't really text Tyler and ask him about it because I don't know our status for sure...UGHHHHHH!!!!

I honestly just think this whole thing with Julie is weird.

I am feeling flush in the face but I am trying to remain calm. I am thankful we are texting and not talking in person so she can't see my face is a little red.

As I think about what she said, a part of me does want to know if it is true.

So, I take a semi deep breath and I text her and say, "Oh cool. What kind

of socks are you both wearing?"
She replies, "I am not telling anyone because I want us to be the only ones matching each other."

My first thought is...*I am so glad she is not going to camp with Mak, Tessa, and me because I really don't think I could put up with her head games all week.*

After the sunglasses fiasco and this whole sock thing I honestly don't really trust her!

She seems to have some kind of problem with me.

I don't know if it is because she is still mad about the sunglasses, or because Mackenzie and I are becoming really close, or because she does really like Tyler!!

But whatever it is...I don't trust her.

I know things can change because there was a time I felt this way about Mackenzie.

But for now, I am going to be polite to her but stay very guarded around her.

I am thinking it is best to keep boys out of all my GFF relationships!

## Sunday

Now that the Academy is over I need to get ready for my girls' golf camp.

I start by going over my mental golf notes in my notebook, so I can work on being more conscious of my thoughts during my golf rounds.

I am really glad we read the mental golf book at the Academy and wrote down our takeaway from each chapter in our journal.

I have some really good thoughts written down that I think will help me.

My mental thoughts from my journal are:

1-Golfers motivated by a desire to master the sport tend to perform better than those whose motivation is to impress other people.

2-People who possess high self-confidence in their skills tend to perform better than those who don't.

3-Don't attempt to try and control your emotions by pretending they don't exist and that you're not nervous. Rather, condition yourself to respond productively when these feelings arise.

4-Focus on things you can control

such as preparing properly, developing a plan for the course and the target for your next shot, rather than things you can't control such as what other players are shooting or the weather.

5-Practice makes permanent rather than perfect, so try to be realistic about what it is you need to work on to get better and how accurately your practice routine reflects these items.

6-Strive to maintain a light grip, because when you tense up you will lose feeling in your extremities and without realizing it, you will grip the club much tighter and hit poor shots as a result.

As I am reading over my notes from each chapter, I realize that all of these points are so true.

I know trying to focus on all of these will be too overwhelming, so I am going to pick one to focus on for my week at girls' golf camp.

I am going to mostly focus on lightening my grip. I think that will help me the most.

Phew! All this thinking, studying, and reading has me worn out!

I think to de-stress I deserve a golf shopping day!

I am going to talk to my mom and ask

her if we can go shopping because I know she is usually up for it.

I have some new bling patterns I found online that I can't wait to try on some new golf clothes.

## Monday

Tessa, Mackenzie, and myself are all excited for girls' golf camp next week.

Mrs. Maureen is familiar with all the ins and outs of the camp and told me that I will be partnering with Mak for the end of camp tournament.

She said in preparation for the camp tournament she wants us to play a few tournaments with the same format. She said, " Playing in this will help you both to make better decisions and play this format better together."

So, Mrs. Maureen and my mom signed Mak and I up for a match play tournament today. It will give us experience with the format and help us gain better decision making for match play.

Mrs. Maureen said it is a much different strategy than stroke play.

And, by actually playing a tournament with this format, it will help us understand when to make the different decisions.

I know it will be good practice for when we play together at the camp tournament, especially for me. But, honestly, every time I play with Mackenzie I always learn so much. She is a really good player!

The tournament we are signed up for is not a junior tournament but a ladies tournament. Ladies often play the low-ball match play format.

Low Ball is sometimes also called Four-ball. The format consists of two teams of two golfers competing directly against each other. Each golfer plays their own ball throughout the round, such that four balls are in play. A team's number of strokes for a given hole is that of the lower scoring team member.

Mrs. Maureen and my mom decide to get a cart, ride together, follow us,

AND WEAR THEIR HATS!

Mak and I are somewhat embarrassed but decided to be thankful we have moms that care about us so much!

Mrs. Maureen kind of knows the two ladies we are competing against today. They are from the country club closest to PWCC.

Mak and I have neither one played the

course we are playing today. But, when we are warming up everyone seems so nice here that we both feel very comfortable!

We tee off on number one and it is a par 5.

Mackenzie and I both hit pretty good tee shots.

On our second shots I hit my ball on the fringe, which is near a waste area.

I probably wasn't going to find my ball.

My mom walked over to help me look for it, and one of the ladies we were playing against came over and said, "UM, MA'AM, YOU ARE NOT A PART OF

THIS!!!" My mom stepped away and was a little upset but mostly confused.

I heard her mumble under her breath as she walked away, "Spectators can help find balls!"

We finished the first hole and Mackenzie actually parred the hole so we won the hole.

YAY Mackenzie!!!!!!

We went to the second hole, and while we were playing my mom saw the marshal. She stopped him to ask him if spectators could help find balls.

He said, "Yes, you can."
My mom explained to him, "Well, the

lady in the green visor said we couldn't.

I was trying to help the pace of play by helping to locate a ball."

He apologized for the ladies' behavior and said, "She is part of the 2% at the club that misbehaves and please don't judge the other 98% of good people here by her behavior."

We proceeded on to play a few more holes. We then came upon a hole where there was a river behind a tree line, to the left of the fairway.

On this hole Mackenzie pulled her ball really hard and it was probably lost in the tree line and it possibly went in the water.

Thankfully, I hit my tee shot right down the middle.

We were getting ready to walk off the tee and one of the ladies said to Mackenzie, "Honey, your ball is OB (out of bounds). You will want to hit another ball." Mackenzie goes to her bag and gets out another ball to hit.

As we are walking off the tee I look to the left and all the stakes marking the water/tree line are red.

I remember from our rules day at camp that a red stake means Mak can find the line where her ball went in and drop a ball and be back in play by adding a stroke.

We get up to Mackenzie's provisional ball and her mom hollers from the cart path and says, "Mak, you have the option to play a lateral or your provisional."

The lady in the green visor, says, "Ma'am, you are not allowed to talk to her!" Mrs. Maureen says, "Look lady, you told her the ball was OB. It is not OB. She played a provisional and has a choice of playing a lateral or the provisional."

The lady jumps in and says, "She did not declare to us before she hit the ball that it was a provisional! She just hit another ball so it is NOW IN PLAY!"

At this point Mrs. Maureen was fuming! I was so glad Mrs. Maureen was on our side because I knew she knew her stuff, and it felt good to be under her protection, and I knew she would handle this.

Mackenzie seemed a little shaken. She looked at her mom and said, "Can I just hit my provisional ball in the fairway?"

Mrs. Maureen said, "Sure!" Mrs. Maureen took her finger and pointed it in the face of the lady in the green visor and said, "Woman, you are crazy!

You already went off on Mrs. Castleberry for helping find a ball and now you are giving false information to these children. You told them the ball is OB, because you are getting beat by them."

Mrs. Maureen was so mad her voice was shaking at this point. Mrs. Maureen then told her, "The Marshal already apologized for YOUR behavior and said YOU are part of the problem group at the club."

The lady became so furious herself (which didn't take much) and Mrs. Maureen looked like she was going to lunge at the lady.

I knew I needed to hit my ball well on this next shot because either way Mak was playing with a penalty stroke on this hole.

Thankfully, I hit my second shot and got on the green in regulation.

For some reason stressful situations like this make me pull my focus in and I somehow play a little better.

I look over at Mrs. Maureen and she was so mad about the ladies' actions that she was turning red and her hands were shaking.

She then told my mom, "I am so ANGRY I better leave before my emotions start to effect the girls. Can you finish following them and we will put our notes together on what the girls need to work on this week?"

My mom told her sure and gave her a hug.

We weren't too far from the clubhouse so Mrs. Maureen hopped out of the cart and walked in.

When the round was over today we did actually end up winning our match against the ladies by 2 holes. And it was a good...but stressful experience.

I feel like if we can handle these uptight ladies, the young girls should be a piece of cake.

One of the best things I learned about stroke play today was that sometimes you go for shots you wouldn't normally go for based on what your partner is lying.

It really is a different mindset and I am glad we played today. I know it is going to help us to play better in our match at the end of camp.

## Tuesday

It's Tuesday and Mackenzie and I have our second match play tournament today. We are playing to give us MORE experience (mainly me) for our tournament at girls' camp.

We also are playing a two-day stroke play tournament tomorrow (Wednesday) and Thursday. Mrs. Maureen found this tournament too and said it is good for us to play as much as possible together even though it is not going to be match play format on Wednesday and Thursday.

I always get a little stressed before a

tournament because I want so badly shoot a low score.

Today, my focus is to concentrate on the shot I am standing over at the time. It's hard because I can't help thinking ahead sometimes.

Today was not a bad round for me. I did better at concentrating.

For tomorrow I am going to focus on my controllables. And one of the things I can control is how I look! So, I am going to pick out my outfits for the next two days.

The first day, I for sure am going to wear a blinged out pink skirt with my yellow polo top with a pink collar with bling on it!

I always feel better when I dress in my one of my favorite golf outfits! And maybe it does help me play better, who knows, but if nothing else it helps me feel better which helps my emotional state!

When I look good, have good equipment and all the paraphernalia a good golfer has, I feel I am controlling some of my controllables and focusing on myself and it just makes me feel better. Now that I look like a good golfer, I need to play like a good golfer.

I know it is a hard sport...but I so badly want to be good!!!!

## Thursday

Today is the second day of our stroke play golf tournament. I was so exhausted after day one of the tournament yesterday. There is no way I had the energy to journal!

Yesterday, I literally came home, showered, and totally collapsed in bed.

To be honest, day one did NOT go well. I am hoping day 2, today, goes better.

I just didn't score very well yesterday.

I did have some bad thoughts going through my head and was gripping the club way too tight!!

Today, I want to try and have fun and work on shooting a lower score than yesterday!

I will hopefully have happy things to write about when I get home today!

Okay, I just got home and today went much better because my expectations of myself were lifted knowing I'm not in the running to win anything, and I was free to just learn and improve as a golfer.

I knew one of the girls I played with today. Her name was Dolly.

Her mom usually gets a cart and rides along with her keeping her score for each hole.

Dolly has been known to write down the wrong score and she doesn't know many of the rules either.

I don't think she intentionally cheats, but I could be wrong.

The other girl I played with today, her name was Nikki. I didn't know her but she finished last after day one.

Today, after I warmed up, I was feeling pretty good about how I was hitting the ball.

We then went to the first tee and Dolly teed off first, then Nikki, then me.

Dolly hit hers a long way, right down the middle. Nikki hits hers way left, behind a tree, and mine was on the left side of the fairway.

Nikki ended up making a 6 on the first hole, I make a 5, and Dolly makes a par, which was a 4.

I was quite surprised that Dolly made a par. Every tournament I've played in with her, I've beaten her.

Maybe she has been working hard and

has really improved.

It scared me a little bit because I didn't want to shoot the worst score for today. I know I shouldn't worry about those things but I do. ☹

After the next few holes were played Dolly had a 1 stroke lead over me. I had no idea what Nikki's score was. But it was safe to say the pressure of being in last place was off of me today.

I did however want to place higher than Dolly!

As we went over to the 8th tee box, which is a par 3, I was down one stroke behind Dolly.

I really wanted to birdie this hole and even everything up between us.

We both hit our tee shots to the left of the green and I ended up making an up and down for par. Dolly hit hers on the green but 2 putted and made bogey.

So, we were are all tied up with the back 9 still to go.

I really tried to stay positive with my mental thoughts and focus on 1 shot at a time.

I tried not to overthink or really look at the scores but it was sooooo hard not to!

When we finished the round and I added up the scores and I did end up beating Dolly by 5 strokes.

However, I think she thought SHE beat ME because as we were walking to turn in our scorecards she said to me, "I can't believe I came in ahead of you!"

I just looked at her puzzled but didn't say anything.

I was hoping her mom had her score right.

I didn't play great today but I know I wrote down our scores correctly for each hole.

We went to turn our scorecards in and

I see Dolly talking to her mom. She looks sad. I know how she feels. Sometimes you feel like you played better than your score. That happens to me quite often.

I was so happy Mackenzie ended up winning the 2-day event today! She works so hard and is such a good golfer. She shot 74,73 for a two-day total of 145.

WAY TO GO MAK!

I feel lucky to have such a great GFF!!!

As soon as I got home today I received a text from Tyler and he asked if Caleb and I wanted to go practice with him at PWCC.

Even though I was exhausted...I will never turn down a chance to be around

Tyler! So I text him back, "OF COURSE!!!!"

For some reason, just being around him, getting a text from him, or thinking about him, I get so happy.

I also get tons of energy and smile...CONSTANTLY!

I wish I didn't get so crazy, but I do!!!

Before we left, Caleb and I grabbed a snack and then started walking to the practice area. As we are approaching, I see Tyler at the putting green.

I also see Julie coming out of the clubhouse and she is waving her hands at me.

We start talking to Tyler and Julie jogs over to where we are.

Before she gets there I ask Tyler, "I wonder if she is okay?"

He replied, "I think so, she was over here on the putting green talking to me about how our socks matched. We both have on white socks. I wear white socks everyday. I have no idea what she is talking about, I just nodded at her and put my ear buds in so I could finish my putting practice."

I chuckle and think to myself...*I KNEW IT!!!*

Julie was trying to make me mad about her and Tyler and this whole matching socks thing.

White socks!!!

Really????!!!!

In that case Caleb, Tyler, Julie and myself all have matching socks on today.

Whatever Julie...WHATEVER!

WHATEVER JULIE

## Sunday

So, Tyler offered to watch Birdie for me while I am at camp. I know Birdie will love staying with him!

He sent me a text when we were on the way home from church this morning. He told me to meet him at the course today at 6pm and he would take Birdie.

He said he is playing in the afternoon and should be finishing up around that time.

He is so amazing!

And, I love that he loves my little doggie too.

I mean, he is the one that made sure I got her!

As it is getting closer to 6 o'clock, Caleb and I get Birdie's leash and start walking to the driving range.

As soon as we are in eyesight of Tyler, Birdie starts whining and whimpering and can't quit pulling on her leash.

Tyler is sitting on a bench by the putting green looking at his phone.

She loves Tyler!

I know she won't miss me at all this

next week while I am at camp.

There is no one else around him on the putting green. He really does spend a lot of time at the course.

That is why he is such a good player.

When he looks up and sees us he hollers out, "Let her off the leash, no one is around."

I am not sure about it because I know how wild she can be, but since there is no one around, I give it a try...and let her off.

Maybe Tyler can train her some for me this week. That way when I get back Birdie will be a well-behaved obedient dog that I can play golf with!

I mean, I want nothing more than for Birdie to be calm and able to walk with me when I play golf.

As soon as I unhooked her leash, she ran right over to Tyler. She hopped up on his lap and started licking his face.

Just then Tyler's mom pulls up in her car to pick him up.

He looks at me with the sweetest eyes and says, "I am glad I got to see you today! I will take good care of her and you have fun at camp this week!"

I am melting!!!!!!!!!

He is so perfect!!!!!!!!!!
And then he puts Birdie on a leash and walks to the car with her.

Who knows, maybe he will have her trained when I get back??

I would love for Birdie to behave and play golf with me!

## Monday

Today is the first day of Girls' Golf CAMP!!!

I. Am. So. Excited!!!

I can't wait to spend the week with my GFF's Mackenzie and Tessa!!

Truthfully, I don't like spending the night away from home, but since I have my GFF's, I know I will be okay.

Things have been going great with all my GFF's, except Julie. She won't be at camp this week so maybe when I get back home, her and I can return our GFF relationship back to normal. Sometimes time and distance fixes things.

But I do know one thing...Mackenzie, Tessa and I are going to have so much fun this week!

After we checked in at the registration table, we riffled through our welcome bags.

In our welcome bags they gave each of us a $25 gift certificate to spend in the pro shop.

We decide to go to the pro shop first and spend our gift certificates before everything gets picked over.

We walk in and right away I see awesome head covers with a sparkly crown embroidered on the top. They have several different colors with the same design.

I can tell we are all thinking the same thing because at the same time we all scream...MATCHING HEAD COVERS!!!!!!

We each grabbed a different color. I picked pink, Tessa picked turquoise, and Mackenzie picked purple.

So not only are we GFF's, we are now GFF's with matching queen head covers.

We decided, for this week, we are going to call ourselves the "Queens" since we have "QUEEN" matching head covers with crowns embroidered on top.

WE even made up a group chat on Instagram and named it "Queens", so we can all 3 message each other and stay in the loop together.

Mackenzie and I are doing everything we can to include Tessa this week because I know it must be hard that she is getting a random partner for the tournament that she doesn't know.
I know camp hasn't really even started but I am already having so much fun!

We are meeting up after lunch today and the camp coaches are going over tee box strategies for ball placement and aim to help us aim away from trouble in the fairways.

I know I am going to learn so much this week!

Who knew there was a strategy to aiming your drive off the tee box!

I usually just put my ball between the markers and aim for the middle of the fairway. I know learning how to analyze the fairway and bunker placement will be very helpful!

Many times tee boxes line you up aiming at a bunker or trouble.

It's the end of the first day of camp and I am so tired...and hungry!

It was 90 degrees outside today. I am ready to sit down and eat in the air conditioning.

I told Mak and Tessa I would meet them in the dining hall because I needed to get my phone off my bunk.

I had to charge it while we were outside because I forgot to plug it in last night.

Mak replied and said, "We will save you

a seat!"

I head back to my room and pick up my phone.
As soon as I pick it up there are 3 texts from Tyler and one video.

I lay down across my bed and I can't stop smiling!!!

He sent me the cutest pictures!!

One of him trying to get Birdie to eat her food, and one of him taking her for a walk.

He sent a video of her riding on his lap in the car on the way to the golf course.

My hearts melts and I feel so weakkkkkkk!!!!!

Tyler is so AMAZING!!!!

Birdie looks so happy! He also texted and said he is letting Birdie sleep with him at night.

He is the best doggie sitter ever!!

I know Tyler has lots of dog experience from working at the Paw Pals Shelter, but he is such an amazing person!

He said they call him the dog whisperer at Paw Pals because he can calm any dog down.

I quickly text him back and tell him, "YOU ARE AWESOME! Birdie is not going to want to come home! You are spoiling her rotten! Thank you for the pictures and videos. They made my day! I am heading to dinner.
I look forward to more pics and videos tomorrow!;)"

When I get to dinner I sit down and I can't stop smiling.

Tessa says, "Why are you so smiley?"

In a high-pitched voice I reply,
"WHAT??? What do you mean?"
She says "Chloe! Spill!!! You have this smirk on your face and you better tell us about it."

I really do want to show Tessa and Mackenzie the pictures and video on my phone of Birdie.

They are so cute!

I mean, Tessa is his sister and Mackenzie says she likes a boy golfer named Jordan now.

I feel like it would be okay to share with them, so I decide to show them.

Tessa makes an AWWWW sound!

Mackenzie smiles and says he is really good with Birdie.

They both look at each other then look at me and say at the same time, "LOVE BIRDS!!!!" And they start laughing!!!

I must have been holding my breath

because I let out a huge exhale and start laughing with them.

I find myself looking around making sure no one else heard it and I also feel so relieved because I really believe, at this moment, Mackenzie is truly over Tyler.

## Wednesday

Yesterday and today were such long days at camp. I was so tired yesterday that I went to my bunk right after dinner and went to sleep. I did not even journal!

I am not used to being in the sun and playing for that many hours a day.

Today, I am SOOOOOO tired again, but am doing a little better.

We have about an hour before dinner and Mackenzie, Tessa and I are hanging out in our room talking. We started talking about an episode of Star

Sisters, our new favorite TV show.

We were talking about the episode where the girls had a slumber party and played a game where they discussed all the boys they knew and then rated them.

We started talking about the boys on the episode and rating them ourselves.

We were laughing so hard! Then Mackenzie says, "We should play! Do y'all want to play?" We keep laughing and nodded our heads yes.

Mackenzie then volunteers to go first. I am so glad she is going first. I would freak if I had to go first!

She says that she wants to talk about Scott first. I thought she would say Jordan, but okay, Scott it is. I am thinking...*I can't wait to hear this*!

She said she thinks Scott is cute but sometime he has BAD B.O. (Body Odor)!

Tessa and I both say EWWWW at the same time.

She then said that he texted her one time and asked her to take a picture of herself kissing her phone screen and send it to him.

Tessa and I say EWWWWW again but even louder.

Mackenzie wants us to help her analyze why he wanted a picture of her kissing her phone and what we think it means.

I comment first and say, "Well, I think it means he wants to kiss you!"

Tessa agrees with me and then asks her, "Did you send the pic to him?"

I am thinking...*I am so glad she asked*

*that question and not me.* Even though I can't wait to hear the answer.

Mackenzie doesn't answer right away, and because of her pause we know she did!

We both scream "MACKENZIE" and cant' stop laughing.

She then quietly nods her head and

then quickly put her hands over her eyes while she is laughing!

Tessa and I start laughing even louder!!!

I then ask, "I thought you liked

Jordan?"

She said she does but she still texts with Scott too.

We finally stop laughing and then the room gets quiet for a minute.

I am staying quiet because I don't want to go next, and Tessa and I are looking at each other.

I am not sure how I feel about talking about Tyler because of Tessa being his sister.

I sit quiet for a minute.

And then, thankfully Tessa says...OOOKAAAAYYYYY!!!!

And HOLY COW!!!!! She goes on and on about how she likes Caleb!!!

How she always tried to be his partner at the Academy, and stand by him.

I can't take it any longer and I holler out, "I KNEW IT!!!!"

She said when she gets a Snapchat from Caleb, she takes Tyler's phone and uses it to take pictures of Caleb's snap. That way Caleb won't see she has a screen shot of it.

She then sends the pic to her phone because she loves having pictures of Caleb's face to look at later or really whenever she wants.

I am trying not to laugh but I can't help it. I bust out laughing.

Honestly, this game has turned in to one big confessional!

After all the information they have both shared, I decide I am going to tell a few things on Tyler.

I tell the girls that I sometimes practice writing my name as Chloe Edwards (since that is Tyler's last name.)

They both bust out laughing at me and start saying out loud...HI, I'M CHLOE EDWARDS!

I don't mind because I feel if I can get away with only saying this...I consider myself lucky.

I then have a thought that panics me. What if they tell Tyler about me doing this? I tell the girls all our information is to stay between the Queens!

We all put our pinkies together and hook them together and say at the same time, "GFF PINKIE PROMISE!"

We all agree to tell no one about any of this.

In my gut, I do feel I can trust them.

After all, they also told some pretty good secrets on themselves, too.

I start to relax since we all agreed to keep things secret.

An hour has passed so we decide to head over to the dining hall to eat dinner.

Today was another totally fun day!

## Thursday

With the big end-of-camp golf tournament today, I had trouble sleeping last night.

The format for today is low ball, which is where we each play our own ball and take the score of whoever made the lowest score on the hole.

I am really hoping I help Mackenzie today.

I think me worrying about Mackenzie, and how my score will impact her, is the main reason I couldn't sleep last night.

Oh, and also because we are playing the Lucy sisters! I am sure that had something to do with it too.

Makenzie has already told me she doesn't care if we win the overall, but she does want to beat the Lucy sisters!

I am going to do my best, but we are playing a longer yardage than I have ever played before. We are playing 5950 yards.

Depending on how far you hit your driver the appropriate yardage you should play is:

| Driver Distance | Appropriate Yardage |
|---|---|
| 275 | 6,700-6,900 |
| 250 | 6,200-6,400 |
| 225 | 5,800-6,000 |
| 200 | 5,200-5,400 |
| 175 | 4,400-4,600 |
| 150 | 3,500-3,700 |
| 125 | 2,800-3,000 |
| 100 | 2,100-2,300 |

So, based on this chart I am going to struggle a little today! I usually hit my driver around 185-200 yards.

I have also been working on some of the tips and corrections I received this week on my swing.

Making these changes has given me some swing inconsistency, and it is worrying me.

I know the corrections will help me long term, but I wish I could get it fixed by today for this match.

Part of me wonders if my nervousness is causing some of my swing issues as well.

I am trying to remember to not tighten my grip on the club, because I know when I am nervous I do tighten my grip.

I am also trying not to have 400 things running through my head, but to pick a couple of things to focus on today.

Oh, and me being nervous about playing well has given me an ulcer in my mouth.

I think I am just so scared I will disappoint Mackenzie and not help her very much.

And, if my lack of contribution is the reason we don't beat the Lucy sisters, I will feel terrible!

I don't want to embarrass myself, but even more, I don't want to embarrass Mackenzie!

I feel like I need more time to work on my swing. I haven't been playing as long as Mak, and it shows!

I get to the driving range and I start to warm up.

I am trying to figure out what I can do to manage my swing for today.

My dad has always told me that before a tournament see how I am hitting it for the day, and play to that.

He always tells me to figure out if it is going straight, a little right, or a little left?? Is it high or low? Whatever you have for the day, aim for the result of that swing.

I know it should be the same each time, but for me it is not, especially when I am nervous!

I figured out that today I am playing a slight fade. So I am going to aim a little left today and go with it.

A "Fade" or "Fade shot" in golf is a shot in which the golf ball curves gently to the right (for a right-handed golfer) during its flight.

I decide to head to the putting green for the remaining 12 minutes of my warm up.

I seem to be putting pretty well today.

I know that putting is half of the game so I take a deep breath and I head to the first tee feeling a little more confident.

I keep breathing deeply and trying to relax as much as I can.

The starter announces Mak's name before mine. She, of course, seems so calm and gets up and hits a great tee shot!

Then it is my turn. The starter announces my name, and I get up to the tee and hit my tee shot.

I actually hit it pretty well.

I am so relieved as I start to walk down the fairway toward my ball.

I don't know why the first tee shot is always so nerve wrecking!!

I think because there are extra people around. I am working on that not bothering me so much.

As I am walking to my ball, I am trying to relax, breathe deeply, and somehow enjoy this.

I have so much anxiety built up that it reminds me of my figure skating days.

The major difference between skating and golf though is that in golf it is up to me to create my own score. It is 100% based on MY performance!

I find golf more refreshing for that reason.

When I was skating competitively, someone may not like my dress, or my music, and I felt I was constantly being judged on things other than my skating!!

My golf score, at least, is all in my control!!

I finish the first hole with a bogey. Mac chipped in for a birdie! I am not too disappointed with my bogey! I keep thinking about our mental golf training from the past month and remain positive!

My goals today for my mental game are: 1. I want to make smart choices to avoid big scores by taking my medicine if I am in trouble, and 2. Avoid 3 putts.

Hurray for me, because on the first hole I avoided both of these.

Each hole I try to make these two mental thoughts my main goals so I can focus on my mental success more than my score.

I play the next few holes with a par, then a bogey, double bogey, then a birdie.

I notice I am not hitting the ball too bad, but because of my slight fade today, I am losing some of my distance.

Because of losing some distance, it leaves me chipping around the green a lot!

I know I need to work on my chipping anyway, so today is good practice for me.

As we are playing each hole, I notice the Lucy sisters and how they really are only concerned about themselves!

They are not worried about talking to us, looking at us, or anything we are doing.

Honestly, I don't mind their style at all because at least they are not playing head games with us!

They are not being rude, but it makes me realize what a self-focused sport golf is.

After the 9$^{th}$ hole we went over our scores with a scorekeeper.

The sister keeping my score put down a

par on the #5 par 3.

UMM HELLO!!! I had a BIRDIE!

I know she knew because after each hole we say our score out loud to each other.

And on hole #5 after I told her I got a

2, she said to me, "Nice Birdie!"

Since she made that comment, I was sure she would write my score down correctly!

Then I start thinking...*why would she write it down wrong?* Is she playing head games with me?

I decide I need to think about the things I can control and pull myself back to positive thinking.

I gently corrected her and told her I had a birdie on that hole and she apologized and corrected it.

But it really did shock me that she didn't write down the right score.

I realize, for my own mental game, I need to calm down and focus on the back nine.

Along with playing the match today I am also trying to keep my stats.

I am working on Fairways hit (FH), Greens in regulation (GIR), putts, sand saves (SS) and up and downs.

Serious golf is really a lot to keep up with when you are trying to be competitive and improve.

You have to manage your food, your thoughts, your swing mechanics, your stats, hydration, and not being impacted by any mind games.

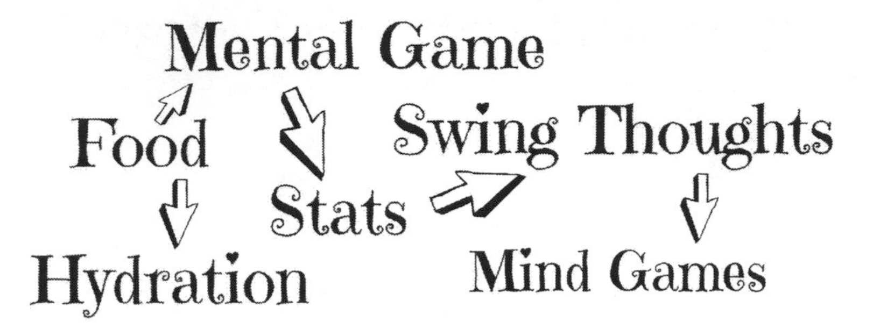


I know it will get easier the more I play, but I have so much to work on, and I have so many areas that need improvement...that it is overwhelming!

We finished the round and I wanted to have scored better than I did.

I have been working so hard, and really felt like I played better than I scored. I ended up shooting an 86 for the day.

I looked at Mackenzie's score and she shot a 74. I don't want to compare myself to her, but it is hard not to sometimes.

At least we did use my score on 3 of the holes. So I did at least contribute.

Our low-ball score was a 71. I just hope that it is lower than the Lucy sisters low ball score!!!

Mackenzie is adding things up and I have my fingers crossed that we will beat them.

While I am waiting on her to figure the scoring out, I decide to look at my stats and see if I had improved any of them.

I notice that I only had 30 putts for

the day. That is a huge improvement for me.

I am learning that golf can be about more than winning. My dad has always told me that in golf EVERYONE loses more than they win, so you must make golf about more than winning and losing.

I knew I wasn't going to have one of

the lowest scores of the day, but I am trying to focus on where I had personal improvement.

Keeping my stats helped me realize I had personal improvement in my putting!

After we signed our scorecards, Mackenzie leans over and says to me, "I really don't care if we win the overall or not, but WE BEAT THE LUCY SISTERS BY ONE!!!" And she gives me a high five.

# Let's Go!!

I don't know if the Lucy sisters have figured out that they lost to us, but as we sit and wait on the scores to be posted on the leader board, I can't stop smiling! I feel like I didn't let Mak down.

I know we would not have shot such a low score if it wasn't for Mackenzie, but it feels good to be part of a good score!

I am watching them write down scores and I don't see anyone as low as ours.

Then I see them write down a 1st by our name.

We hug each other and start jumping up and down!

I didn't expect to win but I am so excited!

Just as Mackenzie and I sit back down, I look over at the Lucy sisters. They cut their eyes over at us and roll their eyes.

Honestly, that does not bother me in the least!!!
We WON!!!

## Friday

This morning when we woke up, the Camp Coaches told us that today is parent pick-up day. That means we have our demonstrations for the parents today.

They hand each one of us a skill that we are going to demonstrate for our families when they arrive.

I look at my card and it says, "The Drive." I ask Tessa what she got and she says, "The chip shot." Mackenzie says, "I got putting, YAY!"

After I got all my stuff packed, I had

some extra time. So, I went and made sure the tee box was ready for my demonstration of the drive.

I filled all the divots with sand, picked up all the used and broken tees, made sure the tee box markers were straight, and then hit a few practice drives.

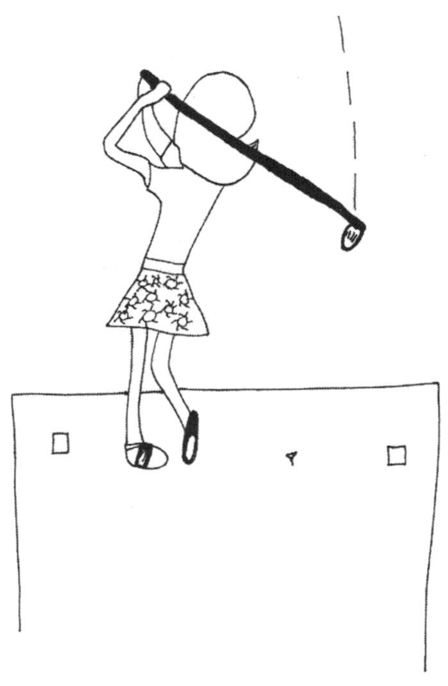

I am really excited to demonstrate my skill today, because I have been driving the ball better since applying the swing tips I got at camp.

I have gained more distance off the tee, and I can't wait to show my family what I have learned.
I think they will see that camp has really helped me improve!

A few times this week, I even hit it further than Mackenzie, and she seemed happy for me!

I love my driver and I feel confident in getting to show the tee shot.

All the parents have arrived, so we start walking to the tee box. The drive is being demonstrated first.

I am so nervous! If nothing else, having this many people watch me should make a regular first tee shot in a tournament seem like not such a big deal.

I want to hit a good tee shot in front of all the people at camp. More than I have ever wanted to hit a good shot off the first tee in a tournament!

I start walking toward the tee box and as I get closer, I see tees scattered everywhere. Like 100's of them!

My first thought is... *the Lucy sisters*!

They are mad about us beating them!

And, they probably want me to look bad!

It has to be them. I am sure they are being sore losers!

But then, one of them jumps up and offers to help pick them up????

I wave her away and say, "Thanks, but there is not enough time."

Her offer confuses me??? Is confusion part of the sabotage??? If so, they are really good at it!!!

I pull my concentration back to my tee shot. I need to concentrate so I can demonstrate a good drive!!

I am going to use some of the mental skills we have been practicing and put all this out of my mind!

CONTROL MY CONTROLLABLES!

I try to act like I am not impacted by the tees scattered all over.

As far as the families know, maybe we were playing a game called throw the tee???

I took my foot and cleared enough space for me to put a tee down.

I step behind the ball and I hit one that carried about 185 yards right down the middle of the fairway and after the roll out it went almost 200 yards!

BAM!!!

Now that I am done hitting, my thoughts go right back to trying to figure out who would have messed up the tee box.

Someone had to see this happen. There are too many eyes and ears around a golf course.

I will find out!

I look around the crowd, looking for my family. I see TYLER...AND BIRDIE!!!! He brought Birdie to camp pick-up.
I run and give him and Birdie both a hug!!!

I then squeeze Birdie and cuddle her as if she were a baby. I am so happy he brought her.

He says to me, "Wow! That was a great tee shot!"

I smile and thank him. I then tell him, "Well, maybe next time we play together at the club junior scramble, I can be more of a contributing partner!"

He winks and says, "Sounds like a plan!"

Tyler, Birdie, and I walk over to watch Tessa do the chipping demonstration.

As we are walking, I reach to take Birdies' leash from Tyler. When I reach for it, he holds onto it too, and we are almost holding hands! He then laces his fingers with mine so we ARE both holding the leash AND holding hands!

I don't move and he doesn't move, but I WANT TO SCREAM!!!!

We are holding hands which means....HE IS MY GBF!!!!!

Tessa does great at the chipping, and Mackenzie, of course, is awesome at her putting demonstration.

To be honest, I am glad I went first because after Tyler held my hand my mind was pretty useless.

All I could think about was I. HAVE. A. GBF!!!

## About the Author:

Gwen Elizabeth Foddrell is from Richmond, Virginia. She is a true animal lover. She loves to play golf, to organize, decorate, and do-it- yourself projects. She loves all things girl like nail polish, heels, and jewelry. Above all Gwen loves God and the people in her life. She loves hanging with her family and friends... and of course she is always up for girl talk!

I want to thank my Mom for staying on me about continuing my writing. I am at a time in my life where my socializing can distract me from the bigger picture. Thank you mom for keeping me on track. I love you!

Bunny
Love
Mad
Maybe
Excited
Feeling it
Done!
Fun
Goofy

Made in United States
Orlando, FL
15 August 2022